A LOOK AT DINOSAURS

ALLOSAURUS

By Nina Theresa

Gareth Stevens Publishing

leveled reader

Please visit our website, www.garethstevens.com. For a free color catalog of all our high-quality books, call toll free 1-800-542-2595 or fax 1-877-542-2596.

Library of Congress Cataloging-in-Publication Data

Theresa, Nina.
Allosaurus / by Nina Theresa.
p. cm. — (A look at dinosaurs)
Includes index.
ISBN 978-1-4824-1819-4 (pbk.)
ISBN 978-1-4824-1817-0 (6-pack)
ISBN 978-1-4824-1818-7 (library binding)
1. Allosaurus — Juvenile literature. I. Title.
QE862.S3 T44 2015
567.912—d23

Published in 2015 by
Gareth Stevens Publishing
111 East 14th Street, Suite 349
New York, NY 10003

Designer: Nicholas Domiano
Editor: Ryan Nagelhout

Illustrations by Jeffrey Mangiat
Science Consultant: Darla Zelenitsky, Ph.D.,
Assistant Professor of Dinosaur Paleontology at the University of Calgary, Canada

Printed in the United States of America

CPSIA compliance information: Batch #CW15GS: For further information contact Gareth Stevens, New York, New York at 1-800-542-2595.

Contents

A Different Lizard 4
At Home. 6
Name Game 8
Big Dino! 10
Body Parts 12
All in the Family. 14
Built to Hunt 16
Meat Eater. 18
Who's Big Al?. 20
Glossary 22
For More Information 23
Index 24

Boldface words appear in the glossary.

A Different Lizard

The *Allosaurus* was a giant dinosaur that lived millions of years ago. Everything we know about them we learned by studying **fossils**. "*Allosaurus*" means "different lizard." What made the *Allosaurus* so different? Read on to find out!

At Home

Allosauruses lived in many places. Scientists have found their fossils in Portugal and Thailand. Many *Allosaurus* fossils have been found in the United States. More than 10,000 *Allosaurus* bones have been found in Utah alone!

Montana
South Dakota
Wyoming
Utah
UNITED STATES
Colorado
New Mexico
Oklahoma
north
west
east
south
Key
= Allosaurus lived here

Name Game

How did the *Allosaurus* get its name? What was so different about it? The bones that made up its back are different from those of other kinds of dinosaurs. These bones had open spaces in them, which made them lighter. Birds have bones like this, too.

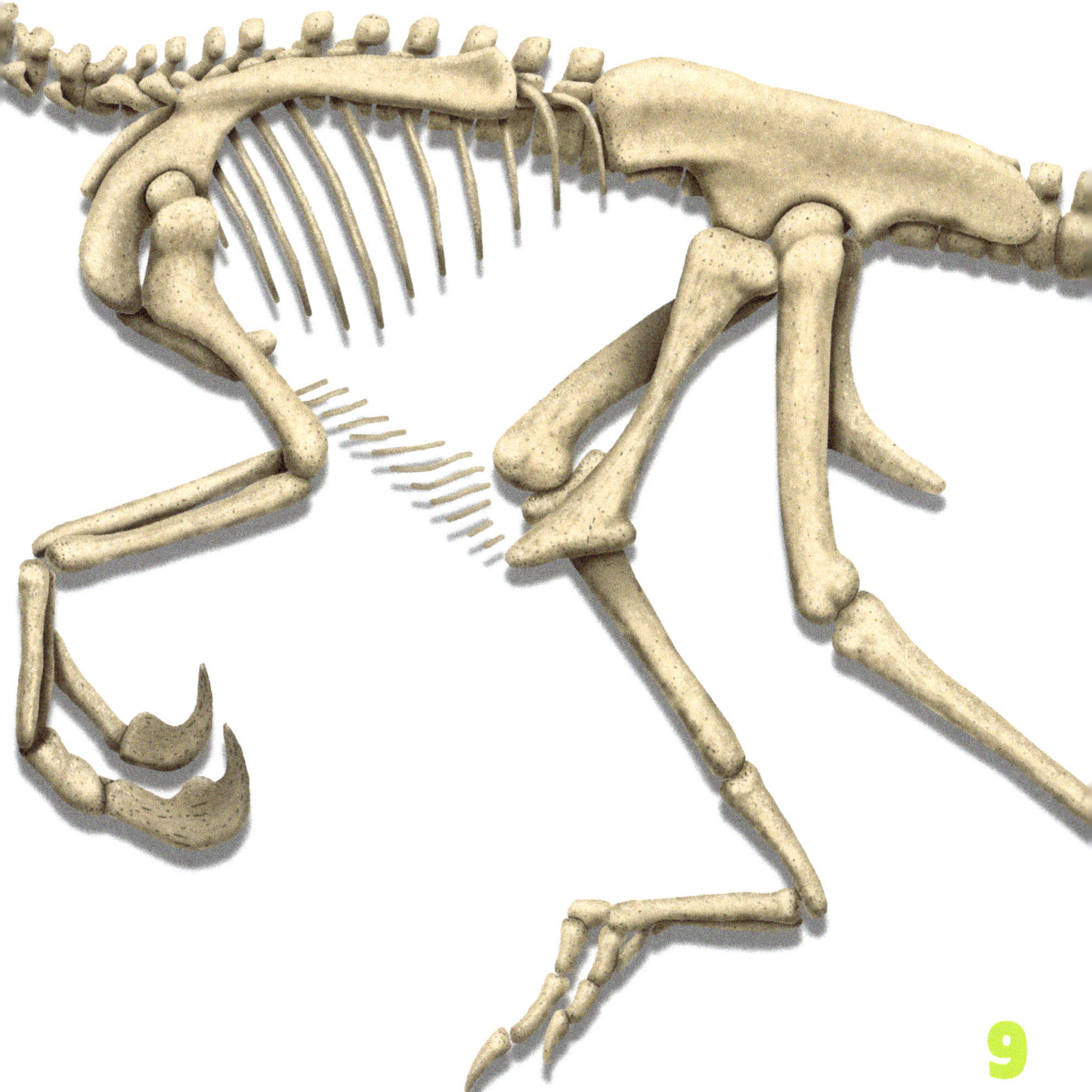

Big Dino!

The *Allosaurus* could grow to about 16.4 feet (5 m) tall. It could grow to about 39 feet (12 m) long. That's about as long as three small cars parked end to end! The *Allosaurus* could weigh up to 6,000 pounds (2,724 kg).

Body Parts

The *Allosaurus* had a large, heavy head. Its long tail helped the dinosaur to keep its **balance**. The *Allosaurus* walked and ran using its large, powerful legs. Its arms were short, but they were powerful, too.

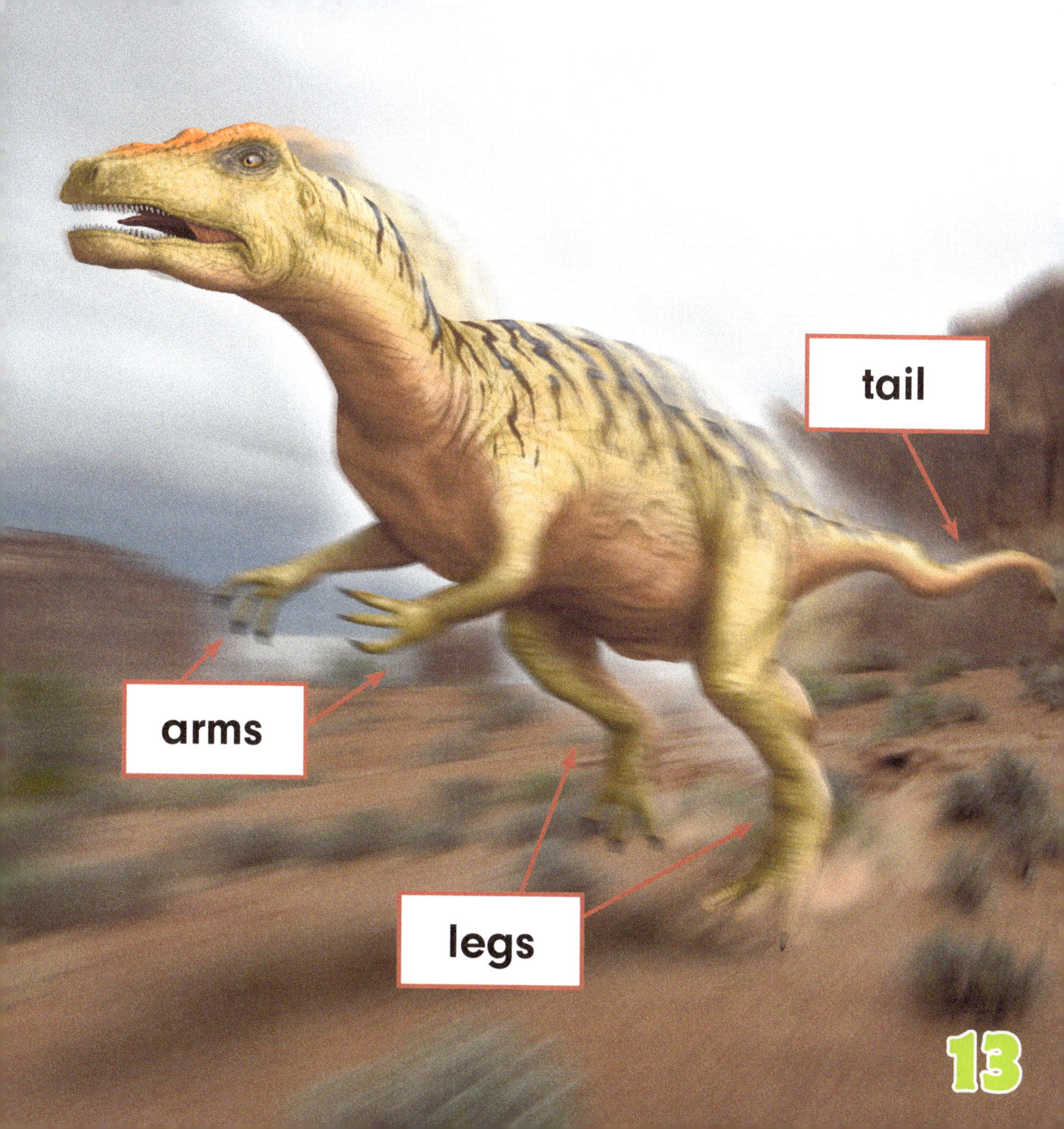
tail
arms
legs

All in the Family

The *Allosaurus* belonged to a group of dinosaurs called theropods. They were all bipedal. That means they walked on two feet. Theropods were also meat eaters. The *Tyrannosaurus rex* is another theropod. Theropods were early **ancestors** of modern birds.

Built to Hunt

The *Allosaurus* was built to hunt! It had three sharp claws on each hand. It used these to grab and hold on to its **prey**. The *Allosaurus* had sharp teeth to tear its prey to pieces. Its teeth curved backwards to stop prey from slipping away.

Meat Eater

The *Allosaurus* usually ate large plant-eating dinosaurs, such as another dinosaur called *Diplodocus*. It was very big, and it had a long neck. The *Allosaurus* also hunted *Stegosauruses*. *Stegosauruses* ate plants, too, but they were mean fighters with sharp plates on their backs and tails.

Who's Big Al?

Today, you can see *Allosaurus* fossils and bones in **museums**. One of the largest and most complete *Allosaurus* fossils that has been found is named Big Al. You can see a copy of Big Al in a museum at the **University** of Wyoming.

ALLOSAURUS

Glossary

ancestor: an animal that lived before others in its family tree

balance: the ability to stay standing and not fall over

fossil: the hardened marks or remains of plants and animals that formed over thousands or millions of years

museum: a building in which things of interest are displayed

prey: an animal that is hunted by other animals for food

university: a school some people attend after high school

For More Information

Books

Dixon, Dougal. *Everything You Need to Know About Dinosaurs*. New York, NY: Kingfisher, 2012.

Raatma, Lucia. *Allosaurus*. Ann Arbor, MI: Cherry Lake, 2013.

Silverman, Buffy. *Can You Tell a* Tyrannosaurus *from an* Allosaurus*?* Minneapolis, MN: Lerner Publications Company, 2013.

Websites

Allosaurus
walkingwithdinosaurs.com/dinosaurs/detail/allosaurus/
Visit the website for the movie *Walking with Dinosaurs* to learn more about the *Allosaurus* and other dinosaurs.

Allosaurus Dinosaurs
kids-dinosaurs.com/allosaurus.html
Read more about the *Allosaurus*.

Publisher's note to educators and parents: Our editors have carefully reviewed these websites to ensure that they are suitable for students. Many websites change frequently, however, and we cannot guarantee that a site's future contents will continue to meet our high standards of quality and educational value. Be advised that students should be closely supervised whenever they access the Internet.

Index

arms 12
Big Al 20
birds 8, 14
bones 6, 8, 20
claws 16
Diplodocus 18
fossils 4, 6, 20
head 12
legs 12
meat eaters 14
Portugal 6
Stegosauruses 18
tail 12, 18
teeth 16
Thailand 6
theropods 14
Tyrannosaurus rex 14
United States 6